GIRLS' GUIDES

Get Involved!

A Girl's Guide to Volunteering

Erin M. Hovanec

the rosen publishing group's
rosen central
new york

Dedication:
To two amazing women—and two of my favorite "girls"—Laura and Jenn

Get Involved: A Girl's Guide to Volunteering by Erin M. Hovanec
Copyright © The Rosen Publishing Group, Inc.
29 East 21st Street, New York, NY 10010

Library of Congress Cataloging-in-Publication Data

Hovanec, Erin M.
        Get involved! : a girl's guide to volunteering / Erin M. Hovanec.
            p.   cm. — (Girls' guides)
        Includes bibliographical references.
        Summary : Describes the many different types of volunteering available to girls and suggests how to participate, from baby-sitting and first aid to painting murals and keeping the environment clean.
        ISBN 0-8239-2985-X
        1. Voluntarism Juvenile literature.   2. Social action Juvenile literature.
3. Young volunteers Juvenile literature.   4. Girls—Conduct of life Juvenile literature.   [1. Voluntarism.] I. Title.   II. Series.
HN49.V6468   1999
361.3'7--dc21

                                                                                99-25235
                                                                                CIP

Manufactured in the United States of America

Contents

About This Book

The middle school years are like a roller coaster—wild and scary but also fun and way cool. One minute you're way, way up there, and the next minute you're plunging down into the depths. Not surprisingly, sometimes you may find yourself feeling confused and lost. Not to worry though. Just like on a roller-coaster ride, at the end of all this crazy middle school stuff, you'll be laughing and screaming and talking about how awesome it all was.

Right now, however, chances are your body is changing so much that it's barely recognizable, your old friends may not share your interests anymore, and your life at school is suddenly hugely complicated. And let's not even get into the whole boy issue. It's a wonder that you can still think straight at all.

Fortunately, reader dear, help is here. This book is your road map. It's also a treasure chest filled with ideas and advice. Armed with this book and with your own inner strength (trust us, you have plenty), you can safely, confidently navigate the twists and turns of your middle school years. It will be tough going, and sometimes you'll wonder if you'll ever get through it. But you—fabulous, powerful, unique you—are up to the task. This book is just a place to start.

It's Your World, After All

It's a rainy Sunday afternoon, and there's nothing to do, as usual. Your best bud isn't around, you've already talked to your crush—twice, and you're flipping through all the TV stations yet again. Your mom asks, "Why don't you get off the couch and find something to do?" for the millionth time.

"I would," you mutter to yourself, "if there was anything worth doing."

You're tired of all the same old stuff. You want to do something that's different, new, definitely exciting, and maybe even a little glamorous. But you have no money, no car—and even if you did, no driver's license—and no ideas.

Dishin' the Dirt on Volunteering

Ever thought about volunteering? Yeah, that's right, volunteering. As a volunteer, you offer your time and talent to an organization that needs it. Two things make volunteering really great.

First, it's a chance to help other people, animals, the environment, your community, or whoever or whatever else you think needs help. You're changing lives and making the world safer, cleaner, and happier. Second, you're sharing your talent, learning a skill, meeting new people, and gaining experience that you can use later when you decide to get a job or go to college. You're both giving and getting, and you're having fun doing it.

And did you know that volunteering is cool? It's come a long way since the days when your mom was sporting a candy striper's pink-and-white uniform. Kids and teens all around the United States and almost everywhere else are working as volunteers for all sorts of causes. *Seventeen* magazine started a contest, the Cover Girl Volunteerism Awards, in 1998. It was their first-ever contest for girls who had made outstanding achievements by volunteering.

Thousands of girls entered, and a few won some pretty fab prizes. Its message:

Volunteering is awesome.

Volunteering isn't just for adults. Kids everywhere are working to make the world a better place. Now is your chance to make things the way you want them to be. This is the world you'll live in for many years to come, so make it an awesome one. After all, as a young person, it's your world.

Stand up, take charge, and do your thing. Don't let anyone tell you that you can't make a difference. Every social movement, great discovery, and amazing invention began with one person's ideas and enthusiasm. It takes only one person to start to change the world. Why can't that person be you?

An Idea, Like What?

By now you're probably thinking, Okay, this sounds pretty cool, but I've never done anything like this before. What can I do?

Lots of things! In fact, almost anything. If you want to help people, you can serve food at a soup kitchen, adopt a grandparent at a local retirement home, or tutor little kids after school. If you'd rather work with animals, you can offer to walk dogs at an animal shelter or pet-sit for a neighbor who's away.

Maybe something in your hometown or city needs to be done. Start a safe baby-sitters club to train other kids and teens in child care and basic first aid, or put your artistic talent to work by painting murals in schools, parks, and other public places. You can help the environment by adopting a stretch of highway to keep clean, making flyers to teach people how to recycle, or planting

7

flowers in an empty spot in your neighborhood.
All you need to be a volunteer is imagination and energy.

So you've decided that volunteering is definitely for you, but you need to know how to get started. That's where this book comes in. It'll show you how to pick a cause and what things to consider when you're choosing. No money, no car, right? That's okay; you don't need them. Next you'll find out what kinds of opportunities are out there and get some ideas for places to volunteer and projects to do.

Once you've decided what you want to do, you'll find tips for getting started and clues on what to expect. If joining an organization isn't for you, think big—start your own volunteer project. Read on to find out how.

Lastly, you'll learn about social activism. Sounds impressive, right? Well, it's easy, and it's not just for adults. Social activists are people who use their skills to solve social problems. Basically it's volunteering taken to the next level. Throughout the book are cool quotes, bios of amazing girl volunteers, neat statistics, and ideas for volunteer projects that can help you get started.

You've got some ideas; you're psyched and ready to go. Think you'd make a great volunteer? You bet you would.

If I can help somebody as I pass along, if I can cheer somebody with a word or song, if I can show somebody he's traveling wrong, then my living will not be in vain.
—Dr. Martin Luther King Jr.

8

Finding the Right Fit

2

Once you decide to volunteer, the most important thing to do is pick a project that works for you. Volunteering is a little bit like dating. Think of all the boys in your class. Lots of them are nice, some of them are pretty cute, but only one or two are really, really fab. Chances are, that one—the one who is the best match—is your crush.

That's the way volunteering works too. Tons of worthwhile organizations and projects are out there, but you need to look for the one that fits you best. And that takes a little work.

It's All About You

The first thing to do when choosing a project is to think about yourself.

What do you like to do?

What don't you like to do?

If you pass through your kitchen only when you're heading out the back door, preparing meals for the elderly or homebound may not be for you. But if you're a budding chef—or want to be—go for it! If the idea of digging in the dirt all day doesn't appeal to you, volunteering at a local park may not be your idea of fun. Maybe you're more of an indoors, like-to-keep-my-hands-clean sort of person.

Would you rather spend the day hanging out or chatting on the phone with your girls?

Put that talent to good use. Organize a "first-friends" program for new students in your school. You and other students can pair off with a new student on his or her first day. Take her around, eat lunch with her, introduce her to people, and make a new friend.

Next, think about your skills and talents.

What kinds of things do you want to learn how to do better?

What are you really good at?

If you've never really progressed past kindergarten finger painting, teaching an art class to little kids probably isn't your best choice. But maybe you're a killer guitarist or piano player. Teach music lessons instead. Or join a community group that paints murals on empty city spaces. Usually no experience is necessary—the people in the group can teach you how to paint. That way you're helping your community and developing a talent at the same time.

The next step is pretty obvious, but here it is: Think about what issues concern you.

What kinds of problems do you want to solve?

What kinds of people do you want to help?

Who or what needs you most?

And with your talents, interests, and abilities, where can you do the most good?

Now comes the practical part. Think about your situation and make a list of your limitations. Money shouldn't be one of them. Volunteers are not usually expected to pay money to assist an organization. You don't normally have to join the group or pay dues simply to help out. If a group requires that you pay them to volunteer, tell your parents immediately and look elsewhere for opportunities.

Stat Chat

Sixty-five percent of all adult volunteers were volunteers as young people.

You'll need to think carefully about distance and transportation. Volunteering somewhere you can walk to and from is ideal, but it isn't always possible. If you're volunteering at your school, make sure that you have a ride home afterward. And if you're planning on working somewhere you'll have to travel to and from by car, ask your parents first. Make sure that they will be able to drive you where and when you need to go. Never walk long distances by yourself or hoof it late at night—it's not safe.

You'll also want to find out about age requirements. Some organizations have a minimum age that they require volunteers to be. If they work with dangerous equipment, such as kitchen knives or gardening tools, the group may insist that all volunteers be above a certain age. That doesn't mean you can't help out; you just may not be able to use particular pieces of equipment or perform certain tasks.

Finally, be realistic about how much time you have to volunteer. It's easy to get excited, be eager to help, and then find yourself offering to spend hours every week volunteering. Figure out how much free time you have and how much of it you want to volunteer. You're better off starting small, just to be safe. If you discover that you have more time than you thought, you can always add extra hours later.

Puttin' It Together

Okay, so you know what you like to do and what you're good at. You've figured out what type of cause you want to assist and what's possible given your age, location, and schedule. Now you need to find an organization to work for. (If you're planning to start your own project, you can read more about that process later.) To discover what's out there, start by looking in the government section of your local phone book. It lists government agencies that fight for all types of causes. If the agency doesn't use volunteers, they may be able to give you information about another group that does.

If you have access to the Internet, go on-line and start surfing. Type in the keyword "volunteer" or a word related to your cause, such as "homeless shelters" or "drug abuse prevention." You can also ask your parents, teachers, and guidance counselors for leads. They probably know of an organization that does exactly what you're looking for or that can help you start your own volunteer project.

For an idea of what's out there and how you can get involved, read on!

"COOL QUOTES" *Set your goals high and work to achieve them and never be afraid of failure, for the tragedy comes not in failing, but in never having tried to excel.*
—Rosalynn Carter (former First Lady of the United States)

One Person at a Time

3

Do you want to make a difference in someone's life? Help a person in need and make a new friend in the process? If you like hanging out, dishing with your friends, and hearing the latest in their lives, think about volunteering one-on-one with someone. Lots of people need extra attention and assistance. Tons of opportunities exist; you can volunteer to spend time with:

Younger People

Just because you're a kid yourself doesn't mean you can't help other kids. Put all your hard-earned wisdom toward helping someone younger.

Teach a group of kids how to use the Internet.

Volunteer's Hall of Fame

Amber Lynn Coffman

When ten-year-old Amber decided she wanted to help the homeless, she wasn't sure what to do. She couldn't offer them shelter, so she decided to feed them. Amber started Happy Helpers for the Homeless and asked restaurants to donate their leftover food to make lunches. Today Amber's group also runs clothing giveaways, works with poor children, and does other things, too. Now sixteen years old, Amber travels across the United States assisting others who want to start volunteer organizations. Happy Helpers for the Homeless now has seven chapters. It is expanding throughout the United States and into Canada and Guam.

Volunteer to be a counselor at a day camp for disadvantaged children.

Teach art, music, dance, or a sport at your local YMCA or YWCA.

Offer to baby-sit, free of charge, for a child who needs extra attention.

Older People

Think your grandparents are the best? Wish you had a couple more of them? Older people have amazing stories to tell. Why not spend your time listening, learning, and making someone else feel loved?

Offer to do a chore for an elderly neighbor. Do the grocery shopping, feed the cat or dog, or water the plants.

Visit a retirement home and write letters for the residents who aren't well enough to write.

Join Meals-on-Wheels, a group that prepares food and delivers it to homebound senior citizens.

Collect books and magazines and give them to a retirement home where they'll be put to good use.

People with HIV and AIDS

Reach out—offer help and hope to someone who may need a new friend. Organizations that work with people with HIV and AIDS can tell you more about the illness and show you all the safety precautions necessary to work with patients.

Attend a party or social gathering at a hospital or home for people with HIV or AIDS.

Become a pen pal by letter or on-line for a hospitalized AIDS patient.

Pass out red ribbons and ask people to wear them in support of AIDS research.

Ask a speaker from an AIDS prevention organization to lecture at your school.

People with Disabilities

People with disabilities, whether physical or emotional, sometimes feel very lonely. A warm smile, helping hand, and friendly chat can make a big difference in someone's life.

Volunteer to help patients at a physical rehabilitation center.

Play games with or read stories to emotionally disturbed children.

Ask libraries and bookstores to donate large-print books or audiotapes for people who have trouble reading or are unable to read.

Organize a buddy system at your school to pair disabled students with other students, who can help them by doing things like carrying their books.

Homeless People

Many homeless people are kids and teens, just like you. Life on the streets can be very hard. Help to make sure that homeless and poor people have what they need.

Offer to help with maintenance and repairs at a homeless shelter.

Plan a clothing drive to collect clothes and blankets to keep homeless people warm.

Build houses with Habitat for Humanity; they'll show you how.

Donate your old toys to a homeless shelter to be used by kids who can't afford to buy toys.

Community Concerns

4 If working one-on-one isn't your thing, think about ways you can help your community. Whether you live in a huge city or a tiny town, there are always things that need to be done. Get to work to make life better for yourself and your family, friends, and neighbors. Make a difference; make your community:

A Safe Place

Keep your streets safe and crime-free. Concerned citizens—like you—can help the police keep criminals away from your community.

If your neighborhood has a Neighborhood Watch program, join it. If not, call your police department to ask about starting one.

Learn self-defense. Then teach others to protect themselves too.

Make a list of useful hotline numbers, like the police, fire department, ambulance service, local drug abuse hotline, and poison control center. Give your friends and neighbors copies of your list.

Become a conflict resolution counselor through your school, church, or youth center.

A Drug-Free Place

Drugs destroy lives. Warn your friends about the dangers of drugs, and protect your family and your community by working to prevent drug abuse.

Contact your local police department. Ask them to start a McGruff or a DARE program (Drug Abuse Resistance Education) in your school.

Volunteer at a drug or alcohol abuse rehabilitation center.

Begin a SADD (Students Against Destructive Decisions) chapter in your school.

Ask your principal to designate your school a Drug-Free Zone. Help post Drug-Free Zone signs.

A Healthy Place

Good health is very important for a long, happy life. By spreading a message of good nutrition, regular exercise, and smart choices, you can keep your community in shape.

Participate in a walk-a-thon or marathon and urge others to join you. Get pledges to support a health-related charity.

Learn how to perform CPR; you could save a life.

Urge your school to offer sexual education classes or to invite a speaker to talk about safe sex and sexual decision making.

Join the Red Cross.

A Pretty Place

Does your town have empty lots, run-down buildings, or poorly kept parks? Make the place where you live beautiful. Be proud of your town and work to keep it clean and attractive.

Clean up or repair a children's playground.

Plant a garden in an empty lot for neighbors to enjoy.

Organize a group of people to pick up litter from the streets.

Adopt a stretch of local highway and pledge to keep it clean and well maintained.

22

This Wide, Wide World

5

What if you want to do things in a big way? I mean a really, really big way. Well, anything is possible, and that includes changing the world. Some global causes start small—locally. But they are part of a worldwide effort to make something happen. Join people from around the globe to create:

A Just World

When you want to make things happen, some people say that you should go straight to the top. When you're talking about world issues, that means the government.

Go door-to-door to register voters. Make sure that an adult accompanies you.

Campaign for a politician running for a local, state, or federal office.

Organize a letter-writing campaign to urge a politician to support an issue that you care about.

Call your juvenile court system and find out if they have a Kids in Court program. This program uses older kids who have been in court to help younger kids who will be going to court. If a program doesn't exist, help to start one.

A Respectful World

How often do you think about civil rights? Probably not too often. Civil rights make sure that a person will be treated fairly by the law and by others. Basically they ensure that people show tolerance and understanding toward each other. Most people take these things for granted, but civil rights have to be carefully protected. Help to keep the world a fair, just, and respectful place.

Learn and teach others about holidays celebrated by people of different cultures, like Kwanzaa, Chinese New Year, and Yom Kippur. Celebrate these holidays.

Tutor a child who is learning to speak English.

Ask your history or social studies teacher to spend one class allowing students to share their ethnic backgrounds with one another. Ask each student what makes his or her personal history special.

Become a pen pal by letter or on-line with a girl in another country.

A Literate World

By teaching someone to read, you can open up a whole new world for her. Share your knowledge. Help someone become independent and start her down the path to success.

Plan a reading hour for children at a local school or library.

Join a literacy group and help teach people to read.

Hold a bake sale, car wash, or used-book sale to benefit your local library.

Volunteer at a day care center or preschool. Read aloud to children or teach them to read.

WORLD HUNGER DRIVE

A Well-Fed World

Millions of people go hungry every day. Ever see food thrown away uneaten, either at home, at school, or at a restaurant? There is a lot you can do to feed hungry people in your community and beyond.

Help to make sure that food gets from the people who have it to the people who need it.

Volunteer at a food bank, which gives food to families who can't afford to buy it.

Hold a holiday food drive. Ask family, friends, and neighbors to donate food to be given to poor families.

Ask restaurants to donate their leftover food to food banks and homeless shelters.

Start a campaign to raise money for starving people in another country.

A Humane World

Crazy about animals? They need help too. If you're more into dogs, cats, and other creatures than people, put your interest to work. They may not be able to say thank you, but you'll know when they're happy.

Ask some friends to share the cost and adopt an animal at your local zoo. You may even be able to volunteer with your animal (depending upon what kind of animal you adopt) by doing things like cleaning the pens, helping with feeding, and fund-raising.

Volunteer at a local animal shelter to clean cages, feed and walk animals, and give dogs and cats all the love and attention they need.

Help find shelters for homeless animals. Or if you can, find them homes.

Refuse to buy products made from or tested on animals.

A Green World

It may be your world, but it's just on loan. You know that you have to leave it in good shape, right? If you like to be

outside—hiking, picnicking, sailing, or whatever—you know how important protecting the environment is. You'll want to make sure that it'll be around for your kids to enjoy too.

Gather a group of people to plant trees for Arbor Day. If you join the National Arbor Day Foundation, they'll send you the young trees for free.

Start an environmental club or earth club at your school to raise awareness for environmental issues.

Organize a car pool program to reduce air pollution.

Start a compost pile to dispose of natural waste like food. Encourage other people to start their own as well.

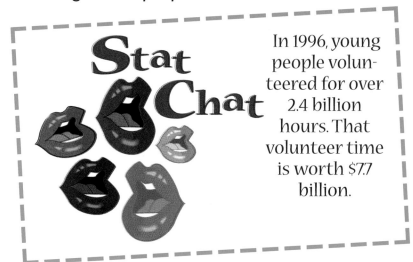

Stat Chat

In 1996, young people volunteered for over 2.4 billion hours. That volunteer time is worth $7.7 billion.

Take It to the Streets

You've found a cause—something fun and meaningful and exciting. Great! Now you're ready to put your ideas into action. If you've decided to volunteer with an organization, which is a cool way to get started, read on.

Hello, My Name Is...

The first thing you'll want to do is contact the organization. You can do this by letter, e-mail, or phone. If the telephone is your best bud (next to your girls, of course), give the organization a call. But before you call, write down a list of questions to ask so you won't forget them when you're on the phone.

Ready? Pick up, dial, and do your thing.

When a person answers, tell him or her your name and explain that you are interested in volunteering for the organization.

Volunteer's Hall of Fame

La-Keé-A Lowry

When La-Keé-A found out that her neighborhood library didn't have enough money to stay open, she knew that she had to do something. La-Keé-A asked students and teachers in her high school to sign a petition to keep the library open. She organized a sit-in in front of the library to protest its closing. She also wrote letters to politicians, including the mayor of New York City, members of Congress, and the president. Because of La-Keé-A, the library stayed open. It even got the money to buy new books and computers. First Lady Barbara Bush invited La-Keé-A to visit the White House. Now a college student, La-Keé-A is still working to promote literacy.

He or she will probably pass you on to someone whose job is to organize the volunteers. This person is sometimes called a coordinator. Again, tell this person your name and explain that you are interested in volunteering. You know the drill! Be prepared to explain why you want to volunteer, because the coordinator may ask. He or she may offer to mail you information about the organization. If this happens, thank the coordinator and get ready to do this all over again after you've received and read the info.

Next the coordinator will ask you some questions about yourself.

If you're the kind of person that the organization is looking for, the coordinator will invite you to be a volunteer and set up your first session.

Coordinator's Questions

Why are you interested in volunteering?

What things do you like to do?

How old are you?

You have some key questions to ask.

The reason you're going crazy with the questions is this: You need to understand exactly what the organization expects of you. And the coordinator needs to know exactly what you're willing and able to do. This way there won't be any misunderstandings or confusion later on.

Listen carefully as the coordinator answers your questions. Write down everything and repeat it back to the person to be sure you've got it right.

When all your questions have been answered and

Your Questions

Where should you go to volunteer?

When?

Who should you ask for when you get there? How do you contact that person in case you're going to be late or can't make it?

What should you wear? Should you bring anything with you?

What will you be doing?

For how long?

Should you plan a schedule for volunteering sessions or can you do it whenever you want?

How much time will they expect from you as a volunteer?

32

everything is ready to go for your first day, it's time to hang up. Thank the person. Make sure that you know the coordinator's name in case you ever need to speak with him or her again.

Doin' the Do

The big day arrives! You may need to bring your mom or dad with you on your first day. Because you are a minor, a person under eighteen years old, your mom or dad may have to sign a consent form. This form says that a parent is allowing you to participate in volunteer activities at the organization. Either you or your parent will also have to fill out another form. On this paper, you'll have to write down whom the organization should call if there is an emergency or if you become sick or get hurt. Have your mom or dad's name, address, and work and home phone numbers handy.

Be on time. 'Nuff said. And if you're going to be late or can't make it at all, call the coordinator or contact person. The organization is counting on your being there.

Be sure to dress appropriately. If you're going to be digging in the dirt or chasing after little kids all afternoon, today may not be the day to try out those cute new platforms. But if you're handing out campaign flyers for a politician or going to a party to raise money for people with HIV or AIDS, platforms are probably perfect.

Once you arrive, the coordinator or person in charge will explain some rules that you'll have to follow. If the rules aren't clear, ask questions. Then do exactly as you've been told. Volunteering is very serious business. If you have any sort of problem during the day, tell the coordinator. Don't be embarrassed to ask for help. You're new, and you're learning—everybody knows that.

When the day or event is over, wait until everything is finished before you leave. Sometimes that means helping to clean up or put supplies away. Ask the coordinator if it's okay for you to leave. Make sure that someone else knows that you are leaving. You don't want everyone looking for you when you're already halfway home! Say good-bye to the people you met, thank the coordinator, and arrange your next volunteer session.

One last thing. You're a new volunteer, and new things are often hard. If your first day wasn't perfect or as fun or easy as you had hoped, give it another try. Sometimes it takes a few sessions to feel really comfortable. The more you do it, the easier, better, and more fun it gets. You'll be a pro in no time.

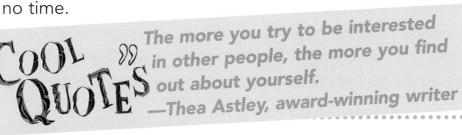

COOL QUOTES *The more you try to be interested in other people, the more you find out about yourself.*
—Thea Astley, award-winning writer

You're in Charge

What if you can't find an organization that does exactly what you want to do? Or what if you just don't want to work for an organization? Maybe you want to be in charge. I can do this, you say to yourself. You're right. You can.

Okay, so you've decided that you want to plan your own volunteer project. How hard can it be? you wonder. Just get a group of people together, pick a project, and do it, right? Well, it's more complicated than that. But this chapter will tell you all you need to know to start your own project. And—good news! You don't know it yet, but you've already done the first step.

#1. Pick a Problem

If you've made it this far in the book, you've probably already picked a cause to support or a problem to solve. If not, flip back to chapter two and take another look. One extra thing to consider: Since you'll be asking others to help you, you'll want to choose a cause that they'll care about too.

#2. Get More Info

Time to hit the books! You'll need to gather information about your issue so that you can tell others about it. You can find information in lots of places: Try the library, the Internet, other volunteer groups, and most important, other people.

For example, let's say you want to work with the elderly, but you're not sure what kind of project you want to do. So you decide to do some homework. You go to the library and check out books on volunteering and on older people and their needs. Then you go on-line and start surfing through cyberspace. You find lots of useful Web sites and click your way through those dealing with volunteering, the elderly, and project ideas. You also check out sites posted by organizations for older people. You discover that individual retirement homes even have their own sites. You see what kinds of things volunteers across the country are doing for the elderly.

Next you pick up the phone and call organizations for the elderly, volunteer groups, and retirement homes. Chapter six gave you tips on good telephone manners—use them now. You explain that you are planning a volunteer project. You ask what kinds of projects that group has sponsored in the past. You also ask what worked and what didn't. Finally, you find out what kinds of projects are most needed. Getting info should be easy and even fun. Most people are happy to talk about a cause that they care about.

#3. Gather a Team

It's time to gather your forces and build a team that can make your idea a reality. You've collected your research; now you can share it. Use your info to show others that this issue is important. Ask them to help you make a difference in people's lives and to make the world a better place. Who could say no to that?

As you're gathering your team, think about each person's skills and abilities. You'll want to include people with all kinds of talents. That way, no matter what you need done, someone will be able to do it.

The best place to start is with your buds. Ask some of your girls to get involved—and maybe some boys, too. Between friends and classmates, you may have everyone you need for a kids-only project. Or you may want to get some adults involved. If you want or need grown-ups on your team, start with your parents and your friends' parents. You can also ask your teachers and other adults at school. If you want lots of people to know about your project, you can contact the staff at newspapers or radio and television stations and ask them to join. Finally, if you're thinking big—really big—get in touch with politicians. You can call or write letters to local politicians like council members or the mayor. Or you can aim even higher and contact your representatives in Congress and the Senate.

#4. Brainstorm!

Once you've assembled a team, put your creativity to work by brainstorming. Brainstorming is a fun, easy way to come up with great ideas. Have a meeting and tell everyone to bring their good ideas along. Ask team members to call out all their project ideas, no matter how silly, crazy, or weird. The rule: There is no such thing as a bad idea. No one is allowed to say anything negative.

When your team is finished brainstorming, the list of ideas should be long. One person—maybe you—will lead the group in discussion. The best way to do this is to pick the top five choices and talk about them. The team will want to pick a project that will help their cause and have a good chance of being successful.

#5. Get the Word Out There

No matter what the size of your project, you'll want people

to know about it. There are lots of ways to tell people about your plan. The best and easiest one? Tell people yourself! Tell everyone you know and ask them to tell others. Have everyone on the team do the same.

You can also get the media involved in your project by calling newspapers, radio stations, and TV stations. This is simplest if you already have people from these organizations on your team. But even if you don't, you can call the media and tell them what you're doing.

You can spread the word around your community by making posters and flyers. Make sure that you get permission from building owners to put them up. You can talk to people in your town and get their opinions by making up a survey or petition. A survey is a list of questions that ask people their thoughts on a specific topic. A petition is a paper that people sign to show they support a cause. If you plan to conduct surveys or petitions, ask an adult to accompany you.

Remember, the more people that know about your project, the more successful it's likely to be.

#6. $$$$$$

Sometimes it costs money to do a project. Raising funds may

even be part of it. For example, you could donate money to a group that really needs it. Or you may need money to pay the costs of the project, like materials and advertising. There are several ways to raise funds. First, you can sell goods. Some groups have garage sales, tag sales, or used-book sales. They donate their own things and ask others to donate too. Then they sell the used items to raise money. You can also sell commercial goods like candy, magazine subscriptions, and stationery. The group makes a little bit of money on every item sold. The rest goes to the company that makes the product.

Or you can sell a service. That means that team members do something for others and get paid. Your service can be a carnival, a car wash, a talent show, lawn care, or snow shoveling. Selling a service is a great way to make money and have a good time. Everyone pitches in to get the job done and has a lot of fun doing it.

Lastly, you can ask for donations for your project. Sometimes individual people, small businesses, or large companies are willing to give money to support a good cause. You can also apply for a grant. A grant is a sum of money put aside by a group, like a foundation or the government, to be donated. Grants usually offer a large amount of money. They are sometimes hard to get, and the application can take a lot of work to put together. But if your project is going to need a lot of money behind it, it's definitely worth trying for a grant.

#7. Just Do It

All of your hard work, time, and effort has paid off. Now comes the fun part. Do your project, whatever it is. After it's over, gather the team again. Talk about how the project went. Was it a success? What worked well? What could have gone better? What have you learned that will help you with a future project? Now is the time to start thinking about what your next project will be!

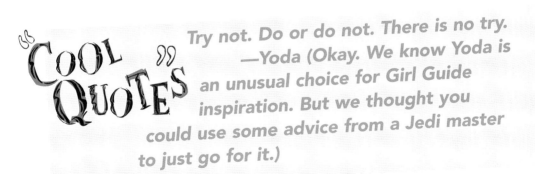

COOL QUOTES

Try not. Do or do not. There is no try.
—Yoda (Okay. We know Yoda is an unusual choice for Girl Guide inspiration. But we thought you could use some advice from a Jedi master to just go for it.)

Social Activism, the Next Step

Crazy about volunteering? Want to do even more? Think about becoming a social activist. It's cool, it's fun, and it's definitely glamorous. Social activism is volunteering taken to the next level. It's volunteering on a larger scale. A social activist works to make changes beyond just her home, classroom, or community. She's got her eye on the world.

Social activists work to solve real problems around the world. Basically, social activists are hyper-committed, supermotivated volunteers. They organize people, raise money, and plan projects that tackle issues of nationwide or global importance. And many of them are regular kids just like you.

Social activists are very important people. They are responsible for many of the things that make your life so awesome. Social activists started the civil rights movement, which gave people of all races equal treatment. They started the women's movement, which gave women the right to vote and to have equal status under the law. Social activists also began the environmental movement, which conserves and protects the earth. They are everywhere, doing everything, and working every day to make your life better.

Want to become one of these people? You're already well on your way! All social activists started as volunteers. To become a social activist, all you need is a strong desire to help people, a willingness to work, and the ability to gather others to join your cause. As today's girl, you're tomorrow's woman. It's never too early to start working for a better world.

What's the Word?

activists   People whose dedication to a particular social or political cause takes priority in their life.

AIDS (acquired immune deficiency syndrome)   A chronic disease caused by the HIV virus that debilitates the immune system, making even the simplest infections life-threatening.

candy stripers   Teenage hospital volunteers who wore pink-striped uniforms.

conflict resolution   A problem-solving technique in which people rationally discuss ways to end an argument that avoid violence and aggression.

coordinator   A person responsible for organizing members of a group to perform a certain activity together.

dues   Membership fees.

grant   Sums of money donated (usually by the government or a private corporation) to a group or organization for a particular purpose and under specific conditions.

homebound   Describes people who are unable to leave their home for health reasons.

organization   A group established to accomplish a specific long-term goal or to provide specific services, usually non-profit.

petition   Formal statement of opinion signed by many people.

self-defense   A specific set of skills that people can learn to protect themselves physically against an attacker.

tolerance   Being sympathetic toward people who have beliefs or practices very different from one's own.

It's a Girl's World:
helpful info

Corporation for National Service
1100 Vermont Avenue NW, 11th
   Floor
Washington, DC 20525
(202) 606-5000
Web site: www.cns.gov

Kids Meeting Kids
380 Riverside Drive
New York, NY 10025
(212) 662-2327

National Council on Youth
   Leadership (NCYL)
1910 West County Road B
Roseville, MN 55113
(612) 631-3672
Web site: www.ncyl.org/home.htm

Youth Service America
1101 15th Street NW
Washington, DC 20005
(202) 296-2992
Web site: www.servenet.org

In Canada
Vancouver Volunteer Centre
#301-3102 Main Street
Vancouver, BC V5T 36J

(604) 875-9144
Web site:
www.vancouver.volunteer.ca

Web Sites
Greenpeace International
http://www.greenpeace.org

Habitat for Humanity International
http://www.habitat.org

The Hunger Project
http://www.thp.org

National Council for Senior
   Citizens
http://www.ncscinc.org

National Crime Prevention Council
http://www.ncpc.org

National Safety Council
http://www.nsc.org

Volunteer Ontario
http://www.voluntario.org

By the Book: *further reading*

DeGeronimo, Theresa. *A Student's Guide to Volunteering: Do the Right Thing.* Orange, CA: Career Horizons Press, 1995.

Erlbach, Arlene. *Kids' Volunteering Book.* Minneapolis, MN: Lerner, 1998.

Lewis, Barbara A. *The Kid's Guide to Service Projects.* Minneapolis, MN: Free Spirit Publishing, 1995.

Lewis, Barbara A. *The Kid's Guide to Social Action.* Minneapolis, MN: Free Spirit Publishing, 1991.

Index

Credits

About the Author:
Erin M. Hovanec is an editor, writer, and former girl. She lives in New York City.

Acknowledgments:
All my thanks to Erica Smith, editrix extraordinaire, and to Laura Murawski for "involving" Ophelia in her marvelous design.

Photo Credits
Cover photo by Thaddeus Harden; p. 6 © Images® copyright 1999 PhotoDisc, Inc.; p. 20 by John Betham; all other photographs by Thaddeus Harden.

Design and Layout
Laura Murawski